£4.75

---------------- GNOWS GNASHER —

PRINT YOUR NAME IN THE SPACE ABOVE AND STICK A PHOTO OF YOURSELF HERE.

— SO GNO GNONSENSE!

© D. C. Thomson & Co., Ltd., 1995. Printed and published by D. C. Thomson & Co., Ltd., 185 Fleet Street, London EC4A 2HS.
ISBN 0-85116-596-6

BEANO BABES
Nº1 BABY DENNIS

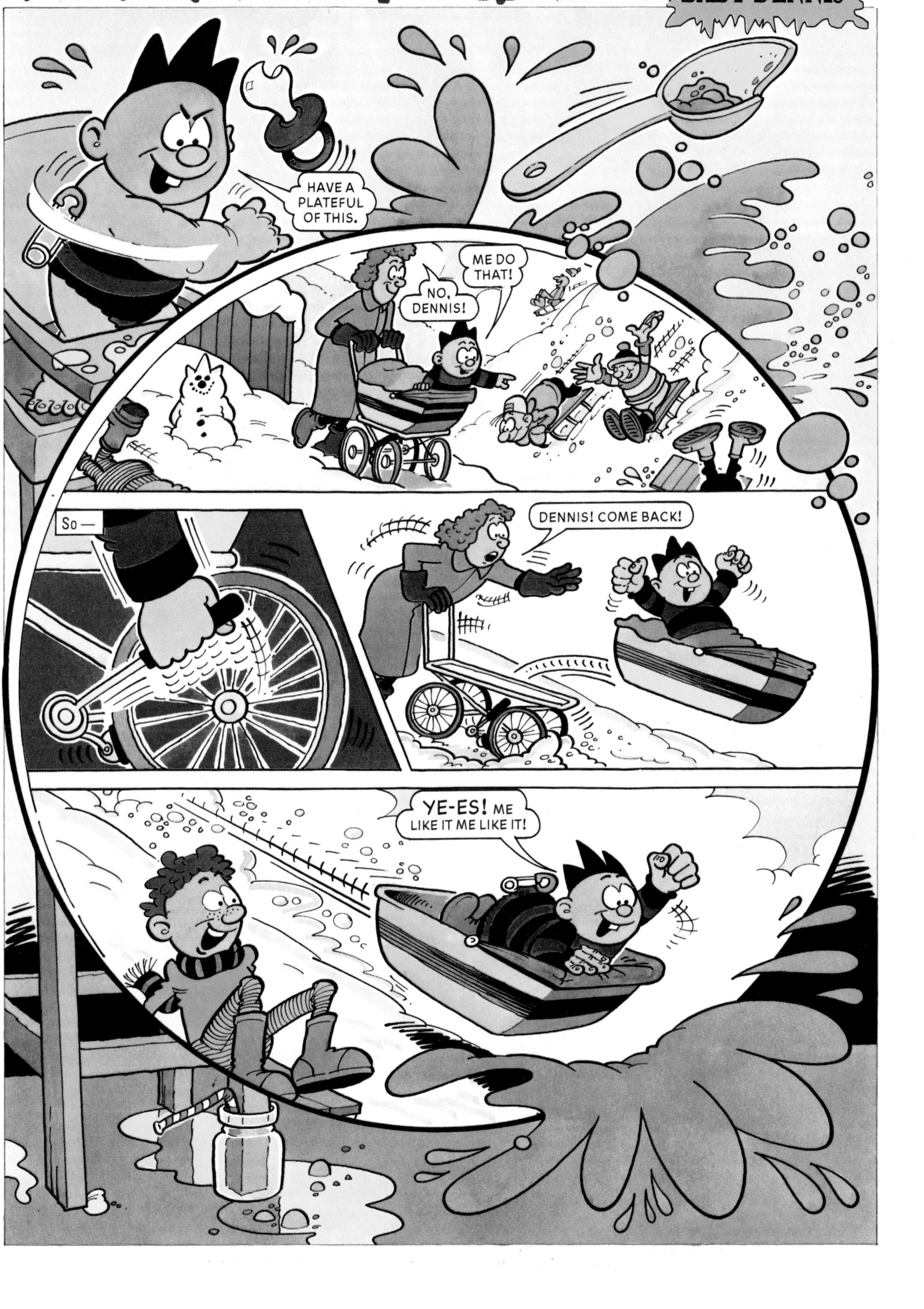

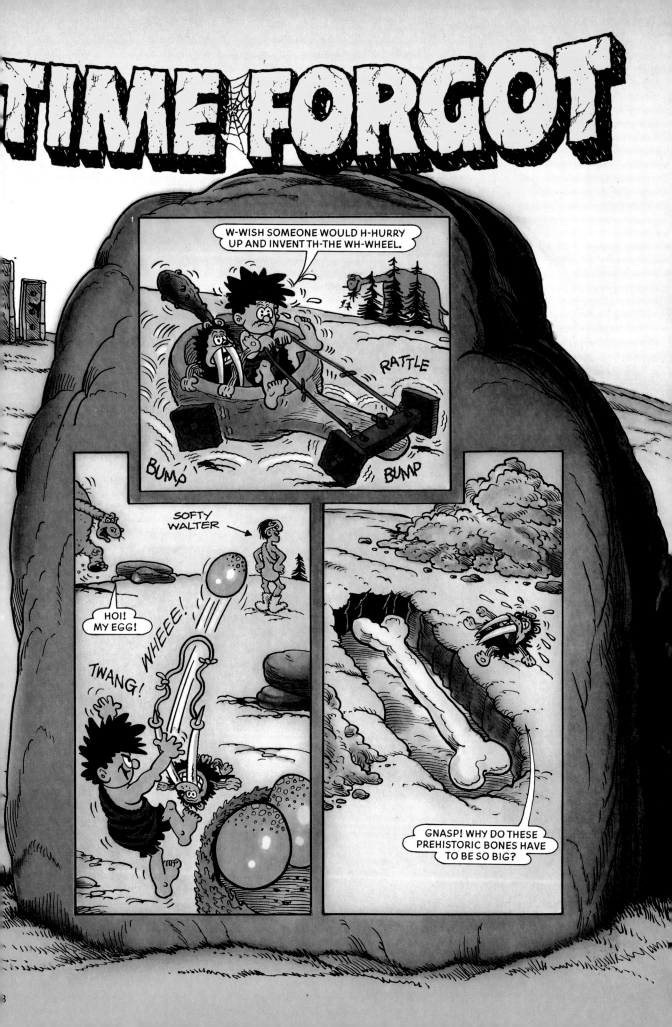

The A to Z OF MINXING with MINNIE the MINX

C is for CORE — that's when eating stops.

D is for DAD who's been to the shops.

PONK!

H is for HOSE to make him keep cool.

SPLOSH!

I's for INGRATITUDE — thankful, Dad's NOT!

A is for APPLE found up a tree.

B is for BITE that's taken by me.

E is for EGG which lands on his head.

F is for FURY — my goodness he's red.

G is for GOOD, I'll help the old fool.

J is for JUMP as he hurls a plant pot.

K is for KEVIN — my what a big lad!

L is for LEFT hook that's landed on Dad.

O is for OUT — my Mum can be mean.

P is for POND where Dad's to get clean.

R is for RAGS as Dad's suit's destroyed.

S is for SACK I get him to wear.

V for VICTORIOUS — number one pest!

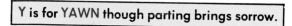

W's WONDERFUL — that's been my day eXcellent minxing in every way.

Y is for YAWN though parting brings sorrow.

Z is for ZZZ! — more minxing tomorrow!

BEANO BABES
Nº2 BABY MINNIE

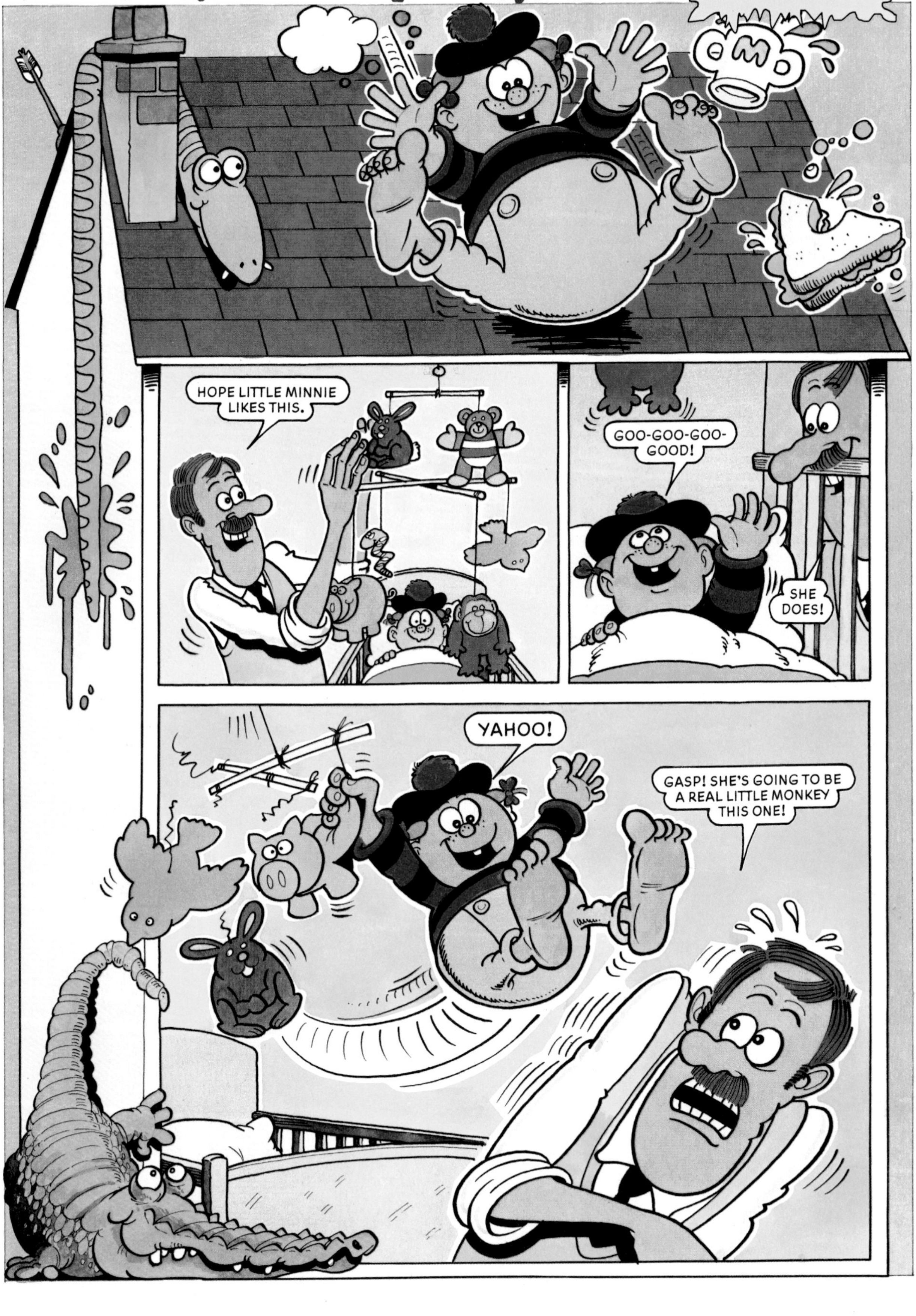

THE NUMSKULLS

CAT'S TALE

Starring Roger's dodge cat, Minnie's cat Chester and a special guest!

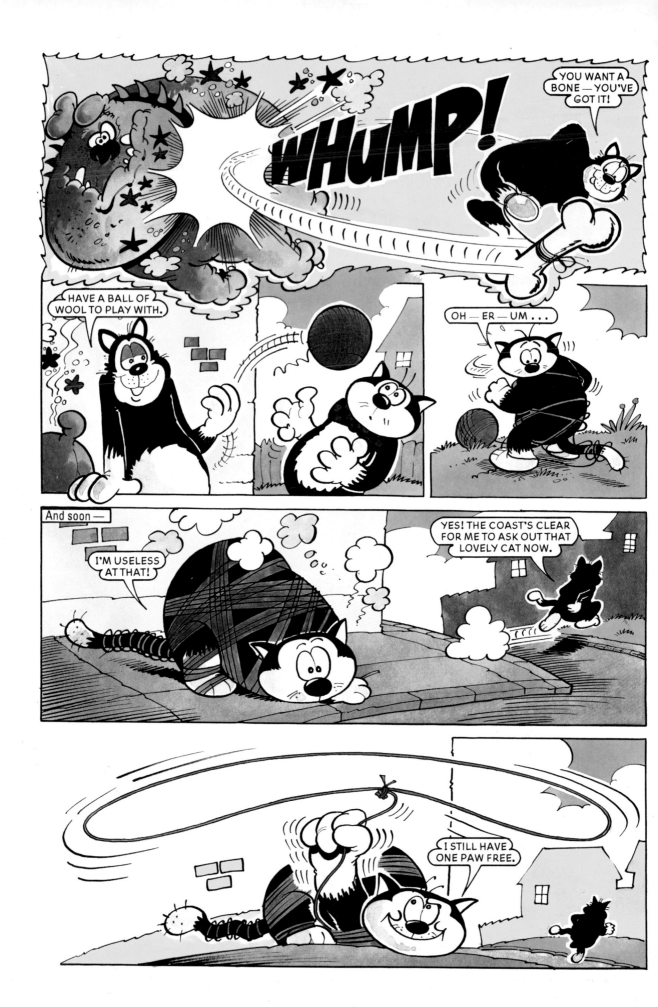

Winston the Bash St janitor's cat.

Sneaky Pete

Crafty Colin

ROGER DODGED US OUT OF OUR SWEETS — LET'S GET HIM!

But—

I'M SAFE IN MY DODGE HUT!

THAT "WALL" IS ACTUALLY A CURTAIN!

OH, NO!

ZOOM!

AND STRAIGHT INTO MY FLUME!

YERK!

CACKLE!

GENERAL JUMBO

JUMBO JOHNSON is the lucky Dinchester schoolboy who has his very own army, navy and airforce of wonderful radio-controlled models.

The young general was on his way to school one morning when his eye was caught by a bill outside the newsagent's . . .

THERE HAVE BEEN A LOT OF REPORTS ABOUT A HUGE BLACK CAT AROUND DINCHESTER RECENTLY.

DINCHESTER COURIER

DINCHESTER PANTHER SIGHTED AGAIN!

Jumbo stopped by the home of his friend, Professor Carter, inventor of the amazing models.

DO YOU THINK THIS PANTHER EXISTS, PROFESSOR?

NO, JUMBO. SOUNDS LIKE NONSENSE TO ME.

GIANT BLACK CAT! SEEN AGAIN

The school wasn't far from Professor Carter's house, and, when Jumbo arrived . . .

SO, YOU'VE GOT A HELICOPTER AS A PET. EH, JUMBO? HO-HO-HO!

EH?

GOSH! I'D FORGOTTEN IT WAS PETS DAY AT THE SCHOOL.

A loud clatter of hooves made both boys turn —

LOOK OUT, JUMBO! IT'S THE BIGGEST . . .

. . . HORSE I'VE EVER SEEN. LUCINDA LAMONT-BROWN'S PET.

YES! THIS IS CHIEFTAIN.

HEY! A THREE DAY EVENT HORSE. BRILLIANT!

Just as Lucinda dismounted, a fierce snarl drew all the attention away from her horse.

GASP! THE DINCHESTER PANTHER! IT DOES EXIST!

L-LOOKS LIKE IT M-MEANS BUSINESS.

EH? KEEN TO GET TO WORK, CHILDREN?

SCREAM!

OH, NO! FORGOT ABOUT POOR GOLDIE.

MUST SCARE OFF THE PANTHER.

His fingers moving expertly over his wrist radio-control, Jumbo 'buzzed' the big cat with his helicopter gunship.

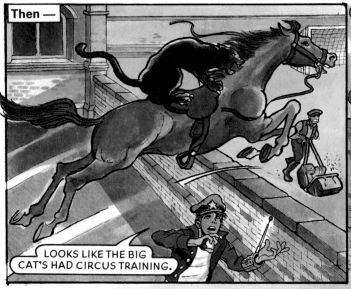

Jumbo pressed a special emergency button on his wrist control.

I'D BETTER CALL UP REINFORCEMENTS.

Jumbo had activated a special long range signal, and in his back garden, some distance away, certain things began to happen automatically . . .

Within seconds . . .

RIGHT, PARAS! INTO ACTION!

GOOD THEY'VE CAUGHT THE REINS.

NOW MY TANKS. GOT TO TIME THIS RIGHT.

EASY, CHIEFTAIN. WHOA, BOY!

At last 'Chieftain' was halted — the small but powerful engines of the tanks held his reins, passed on to them by the paratroops.

ONLY ONE OF THE FOLLOWING UNLIKELY PIGGY FACTS IS TRUE. USE YOUR SKILL OR A WILD GUESS TO FIND OUT WHICH. ANSWER AT THE FOOT OF THE PAGE.

A QUESTION OF PORK

With Dennis's Pet Pig RASHER

1. The Saddleback Pig was so called because, when horse flu devastated Texas in 1874, cowboys had to saddle up porkers to ride about on.

2. Japanese scientists have successfully crossed a pig with a chicken resulting in a hen which lays ham and eggs.

3. A Vietnamese Pot Bellied Pig was named Slimmer of the Year after it shed 12 stone on a diet of swill made from "Quikslim" biscuits.

4. One warthog at Chicago Zoo was so ugly that residents clubbed together to pay for plastic surgery to have him beautified.

5. In the Middle Ages, before street sweepers were invented, pigs were used to clean the streets of refuse.

6. To prove that pigs can fly, eccentric Dutch farmer Hans de Bingbong trained his herd to pilot hang gliders.

CORRECT ANSWER — NUMBER 5.

THE BASH STREET KIDS

WOW! CUTHBERT, THE CLASS GENIUS, IS HAVING A SALE.

LOTS OF BARGAINS.

LET'S HAVE A LOOK!

SALE OF INVENTIONS

THUD!
THUD!

Soon —

WE BOUGHT LOADS OF GREAT STUFF.

LOADS OF MONEEE!

In class —

WHERE ARE PLUG AND WILFRID?

CLUMP
CLUMP
STICK

UP THERE, SIR. USING CUTHBERT'S INVENTION FOR WALKING ON THE CEILING.

COME DOWN AT ONCE!

MINDER BIRD

ALSO STARRING

TERRY the TERROR

WAH! THE ONLY GOOD THING ABOUT TERRY BEING SO LIVELY IS...

GREAT IDEA THIS!

Soon —

UP YOU GET, TERRY!

NOW'S MY CHANCE. HUP...

...AND OVER!

Then —

GENERAL STORE

I WONDER WHAT THE SHOPS ARE LIKE HERE?

CHORTLE! EVERYTHING'S COVERED IN FUR!

GRAB

I DO LIKE THE FURRY BOOTS!

YIP! YIP!

WOW! SORRY!

HOI! THAT'S MY DOG!

GRR!

GRR!

WHIZZ

CHUCKLE!

Suddenly —

TRIP

SPLUSH

GLUMPH!

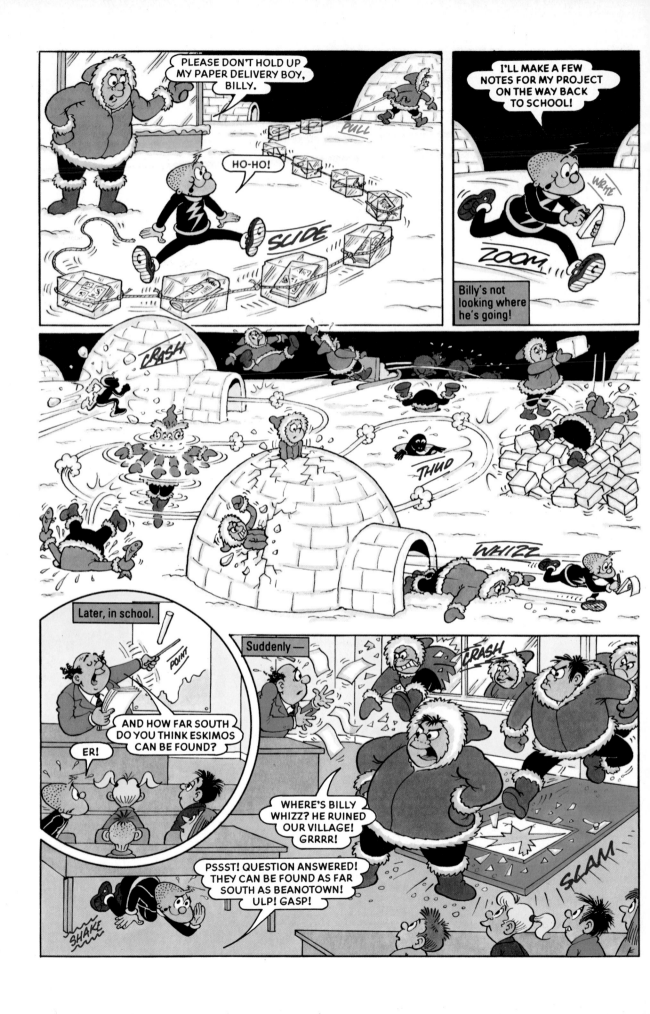

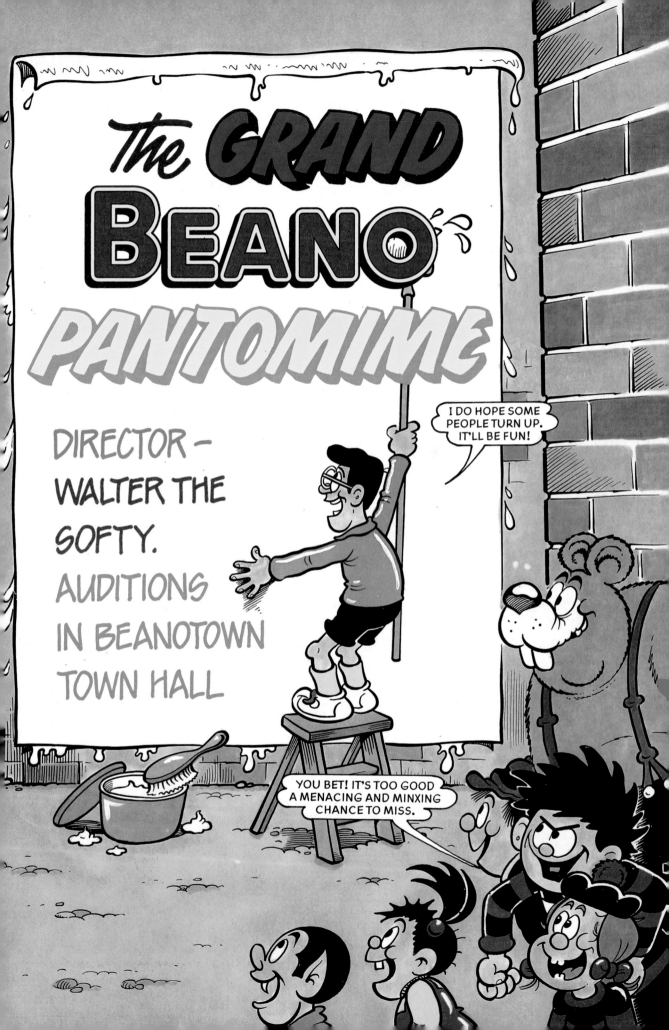

Back to the panto, Readers!

I'M BACK! GET THE TELLY ON.

CHOMP!

Soon—

WHAT A LOVELY BALL! I HAD A GREAT TIME.

ME, TOO! SMASHING!

CLOMP!

SSH!

DING-DONG!

AW WHAT NOW? I'M TRYING TO WATCH THIS.

I'LL GET IT!

YOU SEE, SHE LEFT THIS! I WANT TO FIND HER. SO I'M TRYING EVERYONE IN TOWN. TRY IT, PLEASE!

I'LL TRY IT, PRINCE CHARMING!

Soon—

ME!

ROGER the DODGER

THESE KIDS ARE LATE FOR SCHOOL — THEY NEED A SHORT CUT!

BRIDGE 1 MILE.

SCHOOL

I'VE GOT A DODGE!

TOOLS

THERE!

SCHOOL

FLP!

THANKS, ROGER!

SCHOOL

BALL BOY'S TEAM V BEANOTOWN BOYS CLUB

The game begins —

IS IT THE BALL YOU KICK OR THE MAN — I CAN NEVER REMEMBER.

YEOW!

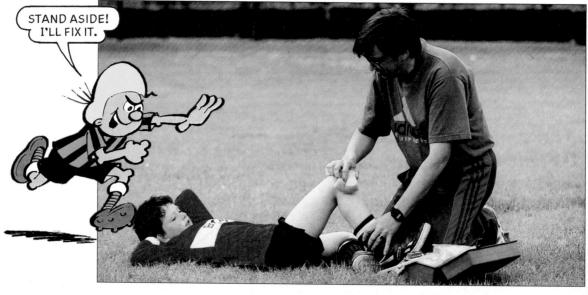

STAND ASIDE! I'LL FIX IT.

So—

SOS! SOS!

SQUARK!

PING!

SOS! SOS! BRIDGE OVER RIVER DESTROYED!

AW! WE WERE ENJOYING OUR GAME.

TIDDLYWINKS

Back at the bridge—

CAN'T GET OVER THE BRIDGE TO DELVIER MY LOAD.

PAVING SLAB Co

S.O.S

GENIUS

I'VE HAD A FLASH OF GENIUS.

STAND ON THIS SLAB, MADAM.

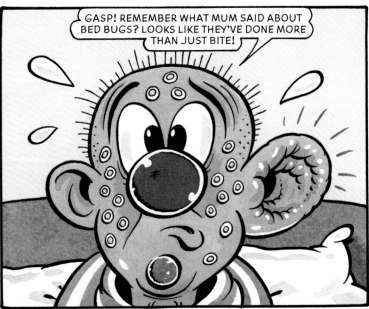

So —

I'LL MAKE BORIS A SKATEBOARD!

And —

YEAH! NOT BAD!

But —

HOI! MY GRAVESTONE!

I WANT IT BACK!

SNATCH!

A GAME OF GOLF, MAYBE?

1ST

DON'T YOU DARE!

BEANO BABES
Nº3 BABY BILLY WHIZZ
LITTLE BABY BILLY GOES THROUGH NAPPIES AT A TREMENDOUS RATE.
IT'S ALSO HARD TO KEEP HIM FROM CRAWLING OUT OF THE GARDEN.
SO I PEG HIM TO THE ROTARY DRIER . . .
. . . AND MY WASHING'S DRY IN MINUTES.

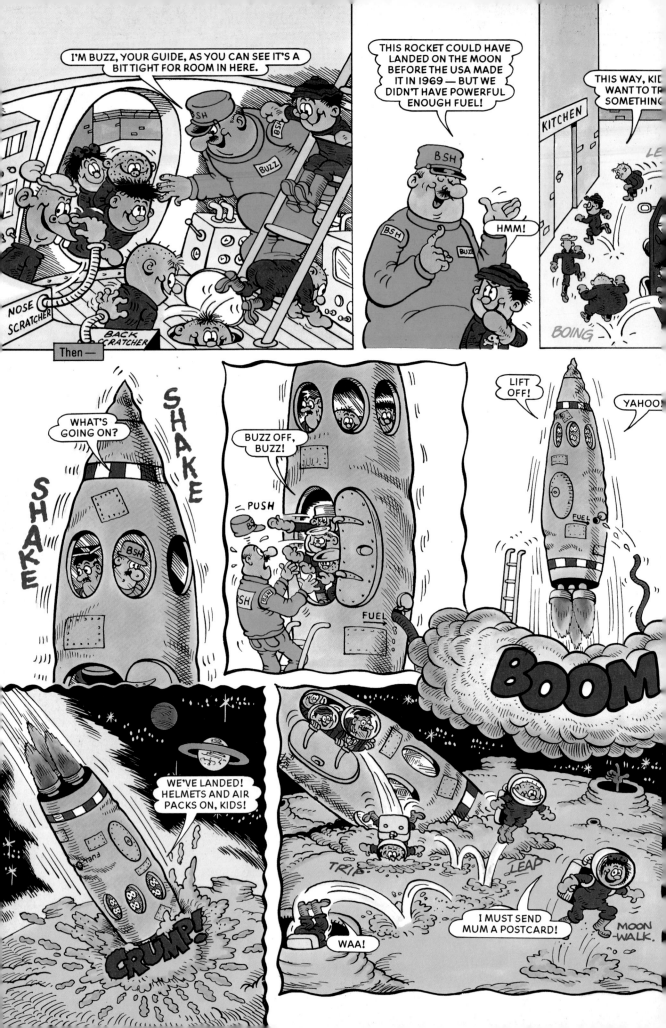

At the top of Smudge's "staircase" —